Andy Builds A PC!

A Fun Guide To Building Your Very Own Personal Computer

By

Kenneth Adams

Book Cover by Kenneth Adams
Illustrations by Kenneth Adams
First Edition 2024

ISBN: 978-1-998552-04-7

<u>Important Note for Parents and Guardians</u>

This book guides children through the process of building a gaming PC. While this can be an educational and fun activity, adult supervision is required throughout the process. Some components are delicate and potentially hazardous if mishandled. Please ensure you oversee each step of the build, especially when dealing with electrical components and sharp edges inside the computer case.

Always prioritize safety over completing the project.

Hi! I'm Andy. You may not know this about me, but I love playing video games, and while I also own a gaming console, I prefer to play my games on a personal computer, or PC.

To date, I've built two machines, and today I'm super excited to show you my process of putting together a gaming PC. It's not overly complicated, but because some of the components are quite sensitive and pricey, you may want to ask Mom or Dad to help you with your build. Remember, safety comes first when working with electronic components!

Are you ready for another learning adventure?

Let's get started!

The first thing to do is to find a space where you can safely assemble your computer.

This project may take you a while to complete, so make sure you pick a spot where you won't interfere with Mom and Dad's daily routine, or where your younger siblings may reach.

You will need enough space to lay out all the tools and different parts of your PC. Ideally, a big enough flat surface, like a desk or table, will work great. Make sure the area is clean and well-lit, too!

Screwdriver

Phillips Head Screwdriver

Flat Head Screwdriver

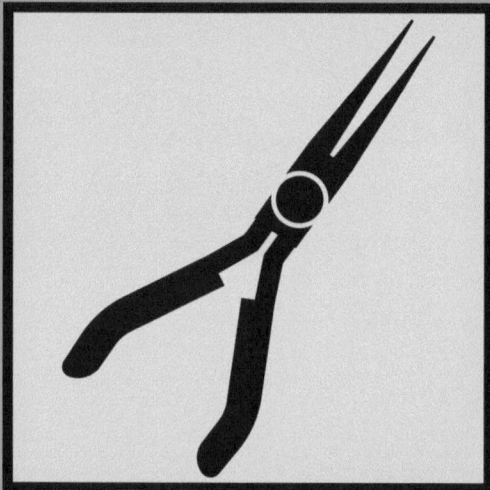

Needle-Nose Pliers

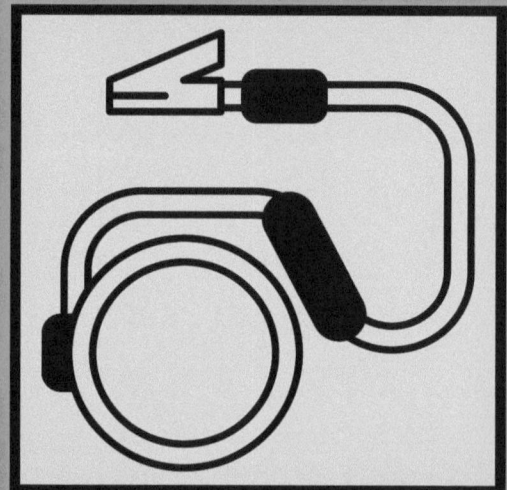

Anti-Static Wrist Strap

Now that we have adequate space to continue, next, make sure you have all the tools necessary to complete the project. In my experience, you will need a screwdriver, needle-nose pliers, and an anti-static wrist strap.

Most often, you will need a screwdriver with a Phillips head. That's the one with pointed edges in the shape of a cross, but you can also make sure to have a flathead screwdriver at hand, just in case.

Needle-nose pliers have a very long nose, and that's why they're also called long-nose pliers. Their long shape makes them useful for reaching into small areas where you're not able to reach with your fingers.

The use of an anti-static wrist strap is very important. Since some PC components, such as the motherboard, are extremely sensitive to electrostatic shock, without the anti-static wrist bands, static electricity from your body may cause damage to these components if you come into contact with them. Always attach the other end of the wrist strap to a metal part of the computer case to keep yourself grounded.

Component	Considerations	
Computer Case	Compatible with Motherboard, Good airflow Enough space	☐
Motherboard	Compatible with CPU Socket, Enough RAM Slots and Ports	☐
Central Processing Unit (CPU)	Speed Number of Cores	☐
Cooling System	Air or Liquid	☐
Memory	Number of Sticks DDR4 or DDR5	☐
Storage	SSD or HDD	☐
Graphics Processing Unit (GPU)	Suitable for Tasks PCIe Power Connectors	☐
Power Supply Unit (PSU)	Adequate Wattage	☐
Operating System (OS)	Windows, Linux, or macOS Installation media	☐

Once you have gathered all the tools, it's time to lay out all the parts of your PC, and there are quite a few of them.

To build a great gaming PC, you need to choose parts that work well together and are fast enough to run your favorite games.

We start with the computer case. The case is like a shell, keeping all the other computer parts safe on the inside

A good case needs lots of airflow to keep everything cool. Some of the better cases have extra built-in cooling fans and dust filters to prevent dust from penetrating the internal components of your PC.

The case should also be big enough to fit the motherboard and all the other components you select. Cases come in different sizes, like Full Tower, Mid Tower, and Mini Tower. For most gaming PCs, a Mid Tower case is a good choice.

The next item is the motherboard. The motherboard is the big board where everything plugs into or connects onto.

Computers made for gaming need a motherboard that can handle plenty of fast memory and has adequate connections for graphics cards. Look for motherboards with features like M.2 slots for fast storage and PCIe 4.0 or 5.0 support for the latest graphics cards.

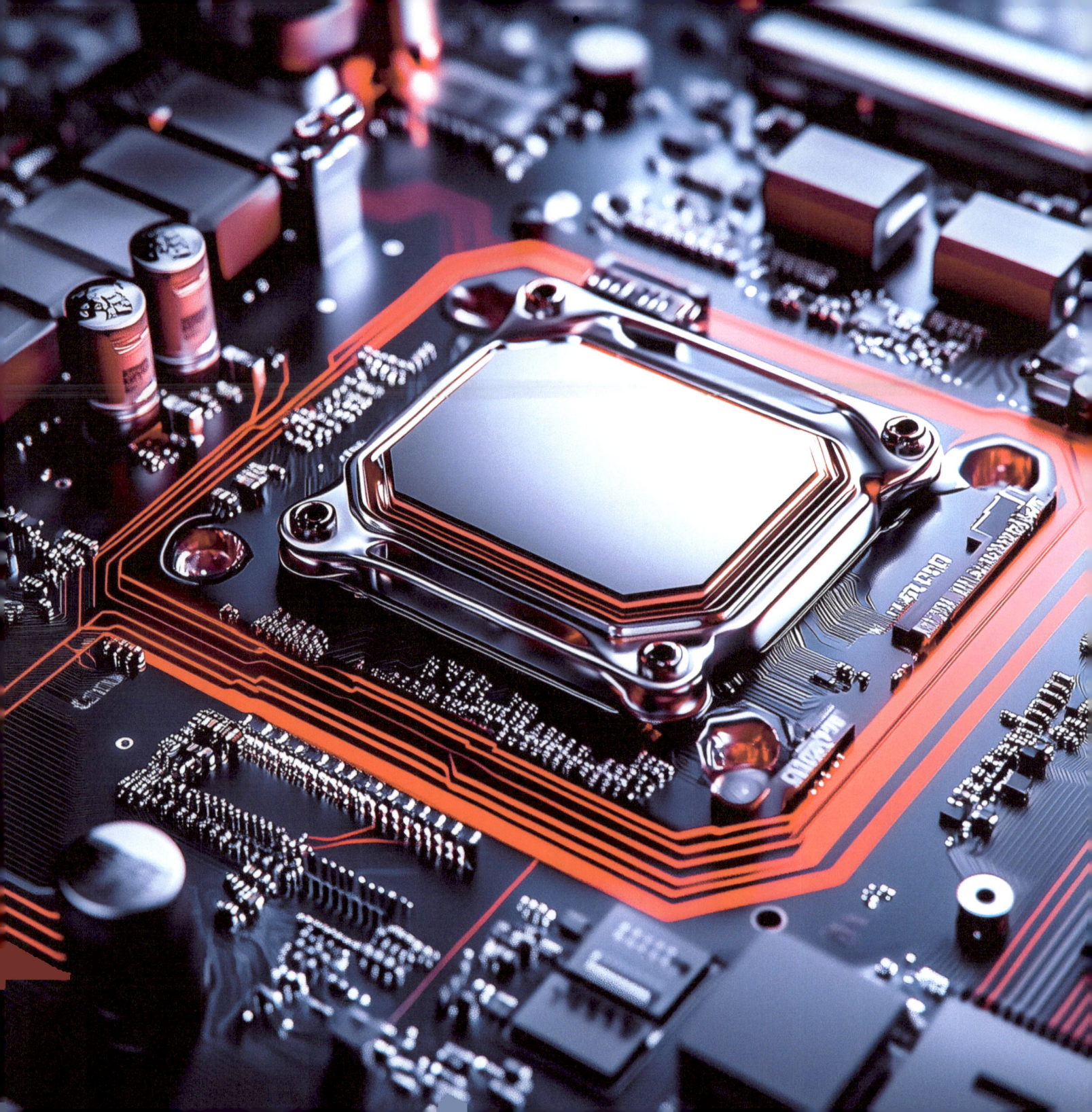

The brain of the computer is the central processing unit or CPU. The CPU controls everything on your PC. When looking for a CPU for a gaming computer, there are several key characteristics to consider, but the clock speed and core count are usually the most important ones.

The clock speed is measured in gigahertz, or GHz, and represents how many cycles a CPU can execute per second. Higher clock speeds generally mean better performance when playing games.

Modern games can utilize multiple cores. Most games benefit from at least six (6) cores, with some taking advantage of eight (8) or more.

I suggest you pick a CPU with lots of cores and high clock speeds. That means it can think super fast and handle lots of game stuff all at once!

An Air-Cooled System

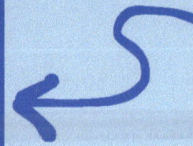

A Liquid-Cooled System

Since the CPU generates a lot of heat when it's working, it is very important to have a cooling system installed to control the temperature inside your PC, to prevent damage to the CPU and other parts.

Most CPUs already come with a built-in cooling system, but it may be beneficial to install additional cooling systems to make sure your PC doesn't overheat and break down.

The two systems most commonly used are air coolers, which consist of a heatsink and fans, and liquid coolers, which consist of a closed-loop system that circulates liquid to cool the CPU. In general, liquid cooling is often better than air cooling, but these systems may be a bit more expensive and more complicated to install.

Always make sure to read and follow the installation instructions, to ensure the components are installed correctly, and to make sure none of the components are damaged during installation. Don't forget to apply thermal paste between the CPU and the cooler for better heat transfer! Some CPUs may come with thermal paste pre-applied to the attached cooler.

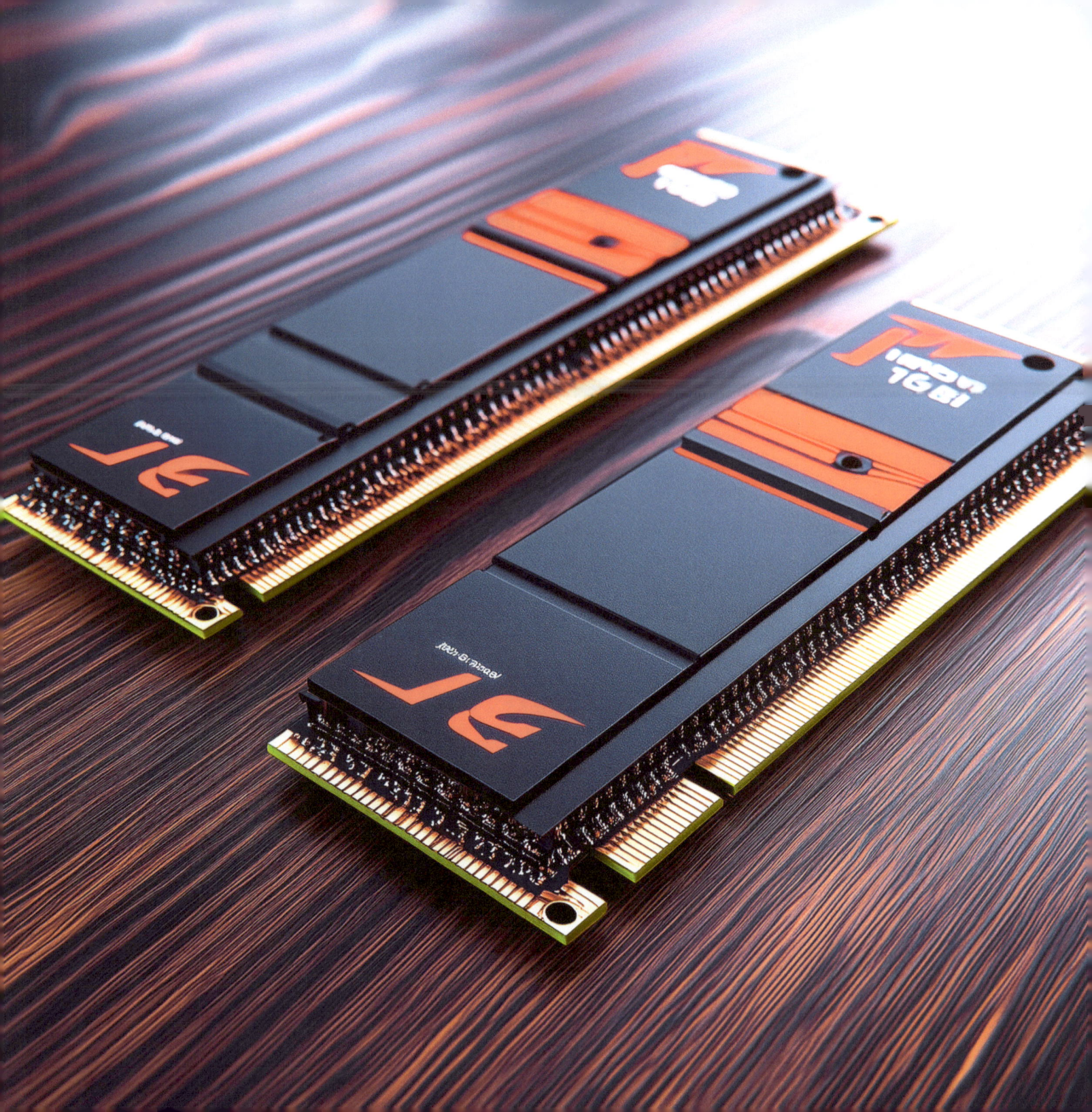

Computer memory helps the games run smoothly. Random-access memory, or RAM, comes in the form of a stick that simply clicks into place inside the motherboard's memory slot. Here's what to look for when selecting memory for your gaming PC:

Capacity: I recommend you have at least 16 gigabytes (GB) of RAM. 32GB is becoming more common and can be beneficial if you plan on using your PC for a long time, without needing to upgrade.

Speed: Select memory with higher megahertz (MHz) ratings. For most current gaming systems, 3200MHz or 3600MHz offers a good balance of performance and cost.

DDR Generation: DDR4 is still widely used and offers great performance. While DDR5 is the newest standard, offering higher potential speeds, it's quite a bit more expensive than DDR4.

Dual Channel: When buying RAM, always use matched pairs of RAM sticks. This means that, if you decide to use 16GB of memory, either use one 16GB memory stick or two 8GB memory sticks.

Compatibility: Always make sure the RAM you use is compatible with your motherboard and CPU. You should be able to tell which type of memory to use by reading the manual that comes with your motherboard and CPU.

Remember, the "best" RAM depends on your specific system configuration, budget, and the type of games you want to play.

A Solid-State Drive (SSD)

An Internal Hard Disk Drive (HDD)

The next item to install is the storage drive. When it comes to storage solutions for gaming PCs, there are several common options, each with its own advantages.

Solid State Drives, or SSDs, connect directly to the motherboard and significantly reduce load times and improve system responsiveness. Non-Volatile Memory Express, or NVMe M.2 SSDs, are the fastest consumer-grade storage options and offer speeds up to 7000 MB/s. Serial Advanced Technology Attachment, or SATA SSDs, while slower than NVMe SSDs, are still much faster than Hard Disk Drives, and offer speeds up to 550 MB/s.

Hard Disk Drives, or HDDs, have a much larger capacity compared to SSDs, but they offer much slower load times.

When selecting your storage, some factors to consider are your available budget, your storage capacity needs, and the speed requirements for the games you plan to play. It's also important to make sure your disk drive is compatible with your motherboard and that there is enough space in your computer case. A common setup is to use a smaller, faster NVMe SSD for your operating system and favorite games, and a larger HDD for storing other files and games you don't play as often.

The graphics processing unit, or GPU, is my favorite part because it makes games look amazing! I usually choose one with lots of memory and power.

Graphics cards can sometimes be expensive, especially when you're looking at the better and faster ones.

It's important to decide what is most important to you. If you want your games to look super realistic, a good graphics card is essential, but if you don't want to spend all your money on a graphics card, a less expensive graphics card can still be adequate for most games out there. Look for features like ray tracing and DLSS (Deep Learning Super Sampling) for the best gaming experience.

Next, we add the power supply unit or PSU. Choosing the right PSU for your PC is very important to make sure it runs well for a long time without needing any upgrades.

Firstly, determine how much power you will need by adding together the amount of power required by each component, like the CPU, GPU, motherboard, drives, and fans. There are some very good online PSU calculators that you can use for this.

Once you've determined the total wattage needed, choose a PSU that provides at least the same amount of power as what you calculated. It's also a good idea to add a little bit extra, say 20% to 30% more, just in case you want to add or upgrade some of the components of your PC at a later date.

For a gaming PC, 650W to 850W is often sufficient. More expensive gaming PCs with powerful GPUs might require 1000W or more. Also look for power supplies with an 80 Plus certification (Bronze, Silver, Gold, or Platinum) for better energy efficiency.

Now, carefully connect all the cables.

Each one has a special job to do. Good cable management helps air flow better, keeping our gaming PC cool and fast.

Group similar cables together using zip ties or velcro straps. Use the dedicated cable routing holes in your case, keep cables away from fans to ensure good airflow, and take your time and be patient. Good cable management makes your PC look neat and helps with cooling!

Once all the cables are connected, we can finally close up the case. Remember to double-check all connections before closing the case!

While your PC is now complete and ready for use, you are not done yet!

You need a couple of other components, called peripherals, before you can play.

You will need a monitor or computer screen, a keyboard, and a mouse.

For the monitor, you will need one with a low response time for fast games.

Choose one that can show lots of colors and has a high refresh rate, which makes movement appear super smooth. Look for features like HDR (High Dynamic Range) for better color and brightness, and consider the resolution (1080p, 1440p, or 4K) based on your GPU's capabilities.

Monitors also come in different sizes. You should pick one that suits your requirements and will fit the desk space where your PC will be set up.

A Mechanical
Gaming Keyboard

A Typical
Gaming Mouse

For a keyboard, I recommend getting a mechanical keyboard for gaming. The keys make a satisfying click and respond really fast when you press them.

There are different types of mechanical switches, like Cherry MX Red for fast typing or Cherry MX Blue for a clicky feel. Try them out to see which you like best!

For the mouse, choose a gaming mouse that fits your hand. Some gaming mice have extra buttons so you can program them for your favorite games. A high dots-per-inch (DPI) sensor will help if you like playing shooter games. Consider factors like weight, wired vs wireless, and ergonomics when choosing your mouse.

Once you've completed connecting the monitor, keyboard, and mouse, it's time to start up your new PC. Setting up the software is the next crucial step.

You may want Mom or Dad to help you with this part. It can sometimes be a bit tricky to understand and follow all the steps.

While there are different ones available, the most commonly used operating system is Microsoft Windows.

On a separate PC or laptop, prepare the installation media by downloading the Windows Media Creation Tool from Microsoft's website. Create a bootable USB drive with the Windows installer by following the instructions on the screen.

Start your newly built PC and enter the BIOS setup. This is usually done by pressing the designated key that will be shown on the monitor during startup. You can leave most settings at their default setting for now and set the boot order to start from your installation media, usually USB, as the first boot device. Save your changes and exit the BIOS setup.

Insert the USB drive containing the operating system boot file into a USB port on your new PC and restart the PC. The PC will now boot from the USB and proceed to install the operating system. Proceed through the installation by responding to the prompts as necessary. Wait for Windows to finalize the installation of the operating system on your PC.

Once the installation is complete, you can proceed to run updates to get the latest patches for software, as well as the latest versions of essential drivers for your computer components. Also, remember that after the OS installation, you might want to return to the BIOS setup to reset the boot order to your main storage drive.

Once the operating system is installed, it is now time to install your favorite games and enjoy hours and hours of gaming, with amazing graphics and super-fast speed!

Always be super-mindful that playing games is not always the best use of your time. Make sure you keep up with your schoolwork and listen to Mom and Dad when they want you to take a break from fighting all those aliens. Remember to take regular breaks, stretch, and look away from the screen every 20 minutes to keep your eyes and body healthy!

It's also very important to stay safe online. Here are some tips:
- Never share personal information like your real name, address, or school online.
- Be kind to others in online games.
- If someone is being mean or makes you uncomfortable, tell your parents.
- Use strong passwords and don't share them with anyone except your parents.
- Ask your parents before downloading any new games.

Remember, staying safe online is just as important as having fun!

Building your own PC is so much fun!

Here are some tips to keep it running smoothly:

- Keep it clean. Dust your PC regularly to prevent overheating.
- Update regularly. Keep your operating system and drivers up to date.
- Be careful what you download. Only get games and programs from trusted sources.
- Back up your data. Save important files to an external drive or cloud storage.
- Monitor temperatures. Use software to check if your PC is running too hot.

Remember, building a PC is just the beginning of your computer adventure. Keep learning and experimenting, and have fun with your new gaming machine!

I bet you can't wait to show all your friends!

www.ingramcontent.com/pod-product-compliance
Lightning Source LLC
LaVergne TN
LVHW072134070426
835513LV00003B/104

9 7 8 1 9 9 8 8 5 5 2 0 4 7